M000201293

Become
M.A.D.E.
It's a Lifestyle

B.O.S.S.
Publishing
Atlanta, GA

Copyright © 2014 by Eldredge Washington

Become M.A.D.E. It's a Lifestyle: How to Live a Good Life by Building Great Relationships. Contact@becomemade.org, www.becomemade.org www.eldredgewashington.com

Paperback - Published 2014

ISBN: 978-0-9863559-0-5

Published by BOSS Publishing

a division of Clay & Clay LLC. P.O. BOX 371612, Decatur, GA 30037

www.BOSS-Publishing.com

All rights reserved. No part of this book may be reproduced or transmitted in any form or by any means, electronic or mechanical, including photocopying, recording, or by any information storage and retrieval system without the written permission of the author, except where permitted by law.

Credits/Acknowledgements

Editors: Mary Render / Janell Braxton / Andrea Paul

Developmental Editor: Howard Clay

Foreword by: Bishop Jim E. Swilley

Cover Photos and Title pages: Tyus Photography

Wardrobe Specialist: Dawn Patrice Consulting LLC

Makeup: Dawn Patrice Consulting LLC

Grooming: Frank "Nitty" Battle/ Kuttsquad King

Photo-shoot Director: BOSS Visions / Emmanuel Johnson

The author wishes to acknowledge that he used pseudonyms, composite characters, approximated dialogue, and some factual events out of chronological order to protect the identities of real-life persons or situations. There is never intent to harm, embarrass, or malign these persons. Parts of this book that could be considered memoir, anecdotal, or autobiographical may be better considered creative nonfiction.

10 9 8 7 6 5 4 3 2 1

Eldredge E. Washington

Become M.A.D.E.

It's a Lifestyle

How to Live a Good Life by Building Great Relationships

Testimonials

"The idea of living a M.A.D.E. Lifestyle is one that forces the reader to step outside of their comfort zone in order to achieve success. Becoming M.A.D.E. has to do with introspection and reflecting on past choices while deliberately making decisions that help you grow and expand as an individual. M.A.D.E. Is a book we recommend to all coming of age readers pick up... It's witty, informative, and personal enough to keep you turning the pages!"

- Andrea Paul, Editor in Chief - B.O.S.S. Magazine

"This book defies categorization! It is a A much needed instruction manual that pushes and prods us all in all the unexpected directions. To become our better selves. You've never read anything quite like this."

- Lloyd W. Sutton, Editor & Chief - Dream Magazine

" Become M.A.D.E. is a lifestyle that is a powerful and motivational tool for future leaders. The keys to success are embedded in each sentence with an inspiring message which guides aspiring leaders to reach their fullest potential by becoming Motivated Adults Developing Excellence."
- *Tamryne Murray, National Co-President- CAR N-Gen*

"Eldredge Washington is a bright beacon of hope for all young people of this generation. I love how his book is based on real examples extracted from his own experiences in life. This book is worth every minute of your time. I am a man in my 30s and I found myself reflecting on my own life as I read this book."
- *Kenshu Aoki, President - Global Peace Youth Corps USA*

"This book should be on the shelf of anyone working with or near children! Who said, "We can't learn anything from young voices?" This book takes, "Each one, teach one" to a whole new level! "Become Made It's a Lifestyle" is a must read for those who would like a blueprint for success".

-Nic Starr, Owner/Artistic Director – Young Voices United
"This book is definitely worth reading. It has helped me examine myself and gave me a new state of mind; Powerful words of wisdom that will inspire all young leaders to live the lifestyle of a M.A.D.E member."
-Bridgette Zulu, Heritage High School Student - M.A.D.E Member

This book is for Winners! I believe that the simple truths presented in this book will revolutionize the way a young person thinks and ultimately equip them with the tools they need in order to be WINNERS in life. Love this book and its step by step guide to building long lasting healthy relationships, it's packed with cutting edge information that will inspire this generation to Change the World in a POSITIVE way.
~ Sam Collier, Founder – No Losing Inc.

Contents

Dedication

This book is dedicated to my parents, Eldredge and Paulette Washington. I am a perfect blend of you both. Everything you love about me comes from my mother, and everything you respect comes from my father. None of this would be possible without your amazing love, care, whoopings, and support. I can honestly say that everything I have ever accomplished in my life was built upon the foundation you have laid in me. Mama, my personality, charisma, and humor comes directly from you. You have taught me the importance of what connecting with motivated people in life will do for you and for that I am forever obliged. Thank you for staying up late listening to me read each chapter and never giving up on me regardless of how distracted I became. You are my mother, friend, and wisest advisor. Thank you for your continued support.

Daddy, my business sense, visionary mindset, and leadership ability came from you. Although everything I have learned from you has not been hands-on, you have lived an extraordinary example that I have adopted and applied to all of my endeavors. I want to thank you for teaching me never to put limits on my dreams. You also taught me to set a high value on myself and that is a lesson most people never learn. I am truly grateful for both of you believing in me. Thank you for helping me become M.A.D.E!

Foreword

Leadership

What is leadership and what is a leader?
It is generally agreed that the one basic definition of
leadership is simply "influence"...it is the description of its
very essence...but there are two quite different schools of
thought about the essence of leaders.

One concept is that leaders are born and not made
and the other is that anyone who so desires can become a
leader if given the right tools.

There is probably a bit of truth to both ideas, but
I do know that with some people, leadership is definitely
innate....something that they are just born with. No one
could have given them that certain something that makes
them influential and no one can take it away from them.
They simply are who they are.

I've known Eldredge since he was around 11 or 12
years old, when he and his very exceptional family began
attending my church, and I can tell you without reservation

(as anyone who knows him can) that, from my observation, he is one of those natural born leaders...influential...wise beyond his years...focused...disciplined...a true visionary. And from what I've heard of his life prior to my meeting him, he apparently always has shown evidence of that kind of innate leadership...the simple but profound gift of being able to influence people.

But he believes that leaders can actually be made, and so he has put his money where his mouth is by creating a workable system of mentoring which proves that the possibility and potential for influence (leadership) lies within everyone...they just need the keys to unlock the gift.

You picked up this book for a reason.

Either you are a leader, or you want to become one, or you want to be a better one than you are.

Whatever the case, you found the right instrument for the

realization of your own personal destiny...easy to read...
relatable...applicable to your life experiences...a reference
book which you will return to again and again. You hold
in your hand here the keys to unlock what already resides
within you so that you, too, can be a person of influence...a
world changer.

Bravo to Mr. Washington for finishing this, his first
book, and congratulations to you for finding it. Now read
it, put the principles to work, and show the world how
awesome you are!

-Jim Earl Swilley Ministries & Metron Community

Chapter
One
Become M.A.D.E

In your life, you will encounter and meet hundreds, maybe even thousands of people. Some of them will be family members, classmates, co-workers, teammates, etc. Regardless of how you meet these people, the relationships you build with them will make some sort of impression on you. Okay, before we get into what M.A.D.E is, let's define the word relationship. A relationship is the connection of two or more people who relate with common desires, ideas, or agendas in which to create an atmosphere to obtain his/her goal.

Do you remember that saying "birds of a feather flock together?" Yeah, I used to hate when my mama said that sarcastically, because she didn't approve of the people I was hanging with at the time. Now that I look back on it, she was unfortunately right! She was basically saying that you are who you hang with, which in my case meant that I was a hard -headed kid, who thought he was a thug because his pants were three sizes too big.

In time, I grew a little older and wiser and became aware that every relationship I create can and will affect me. Whether it's mentally, socially, or spiritually, there will be some form of reaction from your circle of influence.

Everyone in your life can be categorized into what I like to call the three M.A.D.E relationships. The first type of relationship is the mentor. The mentor is someone you may look up to and admire their accomplishments they've made in life. The second type of relationship is the peer; the peer relationship is between you and someone of likeness and you both are striving to reach a certain goal. There is a mutual respect between the both of you because you realize that you can relate in a lot of ways; therefore, you help each other grow. The third type of relationship is the apprentice. This relationship is between you and someone who looks up to you. Usually, the person is younger, maybe a sibling, a little cousin, or someone who lives in your neighborhood. This relationship is sometimes over-looked because you might not consider yourself to be ready, but the truth is that person is watching your every move and you are their mentor.

Birds Of A Feather

Young Eldredge

There may be a few rare exceptions, but everyone in your life can fit into one of these three relationships. What's important is that you learn to create a balance of each relationship you keep. You don't want too many mentors with no peers, or too many apprentices and no mentors. You should keep a good balance of each one around you because they all play a very important role in your life. My whole intention of writing this book is to give you a road map that will navigate you through every relationship you encounter.

So, you may be asking yourself what becoming M.A.D.E has to do with anything? Or, what does it mean? M.A.D.E is an acronym for Motivated Adults Developing Excellence. I started this group when I was in high school. The concept behind M.A.D.E was to get a group of my friends together and we began to do more in life. We wanted to travel, go to college, start businesses, and ultimately change the world. This started as something small and grew into something a lot bigger, hence turning into a nonprofit organization. The main reason why M.A.D.E began to grow was because we were connecting people with common goals and helped them to build strong relationships. Everyone in M.A.D.E shared their dreams, goals and held each other accountable. As a result, most of the members of MADE compared to other students, began accomplishing several tasks, meeting new people, and started becoming more successful in their personal endeavors. How did we do it? Relationships were the keys that unlocked the doors blocking our personal success, but not just any type of relationship, rich ones.

Becoming M.A.D.E is a lifestyle because it requires you to change your entire perception of everyone in your life. It requires you to rise to a higher standard of living, and makes you step out of the social box we tend to comfortably stay in. In the next six chapters, I will give you the formula on how to become M.A.D.E. and provide personal examples using M.A.D.E principles. I will introduce you to relationships that I have formed over the years with hopes of inspiring you to do the same. Certainly, I am not trying to make you be like me or follow the path I chose to take, but I do want to make you think about the people you allow in your life. This is not a book you read one time and anxiously wait for the movie to come out in theaters. It is a book that you read once and continue to reference. If you are not looking for a change in your life and you are satisfied with your circle of influence, please do yourself a favor, and stop reading this book now. I want to form a paradigm shift in your mind that motivates you to build zenith relationships. If this seems like a lifestyle you would like to adopt, I encourage you to continue reading and prepare to embark on this journey of success.

Complete the following exercise. Please use pencil
List 10 people in your life and categorize them into the three
key relationships. Write beside their name M = Mentor, P =
Peer, A = Apprentice.

1._____

2._____

3._____

4._____

5._____

6._____

7._____

8._____

9._____

10._____

Chapter
Two
Become True to Yourself

Now it's time to get to work! You are about to become M.A.D.E! Let's get started by answering these questions. Do you know what you want to do in life? What makes you happy? Before you can build relationships with like-minded people, you have to know what you like. Of course, this might be hard, because who you actually are might not fit what your family or friends want for you. Evaluate everything in your life; the people you hang around, the places you go, and the career you're thinking about pursuing. Why do you like these things? Is it because you are trying to please other people in your circle? It's time to be true to yourself! I don't care if you lose every so called friend you have. If they are not supporting you and your dreams, you do not need them. I know this is something that is easier said than done, but a very necessary step in the process of becoming M.A.D.E.

Alright, don't get me wrong, I am a very practical person. I am not telling you to tell all of your friends you can't hang with them anymore because they are not M.A.D.E. But, I am saying that the longer you keep them around the longer you stunt your growth. Bad friends are like gravity; no one is exempt from the law of gravity. I use to try to hold on to bad relationships because of the history we shared, but I realized that the only thing I was holding back was my future. Success is comprised of choices and sacrifices. Until your friends are ready to make that choice for themselves, you have to sacrifice having them in your life. Do not get discouraged! You may be what they need to get their act together. I have friends that I had to temporarily sacrifice due to where I was going, but now we are connected again. Before, they played the role of a peer in my life, but when I became focused and made the necessary adjustments, they are back in my life as apprentices. My friends are very proud of my progress and desire to do the same in their life. This is an amazing feeling to know that your life affected someone else's in a positive way. By making the decision to be true to yourself, you may change someone's life. Remember, there are always people watching.

I know you're wondering how I did it right? Well, it took time, patience, and strategy. I had to construct a plan of action that allowed me to be honest with who I wanted to be. The first thing I did was create an environment that supported my dreams. I needed some new friends, but I still loved my old ones. We had known each other forever and I couldn't just drop them cold turkey. I established a healthy atmosphere where I could be myself without being judged. I am not old or anything, but when I was trying to make this transition in my life, we didn't have the social networks like

Facebook, Twitter, Instagram, Tumbler, and Meetup. These social media tools make it easy to find groups who support your passion. The only thing I had was a free trial run AOL disk, so unfortunately the internet was no help for me. Back then, my passion was focused on music. Yes, I loved it so much! In my head, I was the hottest rapper alive (big emphasis on in my head). I remembered I had this line that was like "Yeah Yeah Ya boy spit fire I only drink propane, top three rappers me, Luda, then Wayne." In a freestyle cypher people use to love it!

When it came to discovering a place where I could be myself, I still wanted to be around music. I changed my genre and began to do Holy Hip-Hop. Hold on let's stop! Before I move on, I just want to note that this is not a book attempting to get you to change your faith or religion. I am simply giving you examples of how I became M.A.D.E. At that time in my life, being in a Christian setting was best for me. That was the choice I made in order to become true to myself.

The beginning part of your transition is usually the hardest because you are letting things go that you never thought you would. But once you begin to meet new people who have similar goals, it becomes easy. For me, the person who helped me dive in head first was Xavier Gordon aka

X-man. During this stage of my life, we were both members of Church In The Now. We knew about each other, but not on a real personal level. I will never forget the night that I attended a youth explosion at a church in Social Circle, Georgia. A singing group (not very good) got up to sing on stage. They sounded horrible! But, because they were young males singing Gospel, the crowd went wild! Xay and I sat there and watched silently in disbelief at the crowd's reaction. Then he turns to me and says "Hey, you want to start a group?" I was amazed that he asked me because Xay was actually a pretty talented dude. For him to ask me, was an honor and privilege. After a few meetings and phone calls, we decided we wanted to make the group a trio instead of a duet. Xay introduced me to Montay Dickerson aka Levi D a phenomenal lyricist from Dallas Texas. My older brother Nick (maybe the most creative person I know) came up with the name Truth Betold, and instantly I had a new set of friends who supported my dream. Looking back, I see how it all came together. Once I decided to become M.A.D.E, I began to do Holy Hip Hop music. Then I put myself in places that supported that decision, which was the youth explosion in Social Circle. This ultimately opened the door for new relationships with Xay and Montay. The cool thing about those relationships is that they are still thriving to this day. We don't see each other every day, but we do text, call, or hang out on occasion. I even had an opportunity to roommate with both of them at one time.

My point is if you are going to really do this and become M.A.D.E, you have to begin making important changes in life and your surroundings. Think of it like this- you can't plant a seed in gravel and expect it to grow. You need soil. Without the correct climate, the seed will never grow into a tree. The same goes for you. Until you get around a wholesome environment and a positive social group that supports who you are, you will never be able to grow into who you were meant to be.

Steps To Become True To Yourself

Become more confident

Once you learn who you sincerely are, become so planted that no one can change your mind about it.

Become more trusting of your intuition

Your instinct is a reflection of your true desires. Therefore, do not try to silence that little voice in your head. He/she usually knows what's right.

Become the architect of your social circle

Find new friends and build relationships with people who support and believe in your dream.

Become an investor of your passion

Join clubs, attend events, and research groups that will allow you to be who you are.

Become aware of your comfort level

Know your limits. Only you can determine how far you are willing to go. If you're not feeling it, don't to do it. Work at your own pace.

Please complete the following exercise. Please use pencil.

What do you normally do for fun with your friends?

_____

_____

_____

_____

_____

_____

_____

_____

_____

Is this something you honestly like to do or you like being around your friends and just join them?

_____

_____

_____

_____

_____

_____

_____

_____

What is your ultimate goal in life? Does it line up with your current group of friends' goals?

_____

_____

_____

_____

_____

_____

_____

Do you feel you need to create new relationships with people who support your dream?

_____

_____

_____

_____

_____

_____

_____

_____

_____

_____

_____

_____

Do you feel like you are being true to yourself? If not, explain why?

_____

_____

_____

_____

_____

_____

_____

_____

_____

_____

_____

_____

_____

_____

_____

_____

_____

_____

_____

_____

_____

Chapter Three

Become Motivated

How do you become motivated? Motivation is what prompts you to move into something great. Some forms may include your favorite movie, music, a good book, etc. The biggest form of motivation is in your day to day relationships. Have you ever watched a Nascar race before? I was never a big fan, but my Uncle Keith swears he is Jeff Gordon reincarnated. The most interesting component in the race is when the car makes a pit stop. I love the way everyone instantly works on their section to get their car back in the race. This is an awesome example of how your friends should be. Every day you are running the race of life. When you feel you need a break, you have a team of people who are rushing to encourage and make sure you have everything you need.

For me, the next best form of motivation comes through literature. Growing up in a strict holiness church, I was not allowed to watch TV until I was twelve years-old. Seriously! It didn't seem that crazy growing up because my amazing mother (Paulette Washington) was very innovative in always finding clean holiness fun for my siblings and me. As a result, reading became a form of entertainment and a major source of what propels me.

If you were given the opportunity to be mentored by anyone in the world, who would you choose? You can be mentored through their books, articles, blogs, and/or newsletters. When people write, they are sharing knowledge they have obtained throughout their life. I've read, reviewed, and applied almost every book that Jeffrey Gitomer has ever published. He has not only become my favorite author, but also my literature mentor.

Another way, I get motivated is through my environment. I am a native of a small town called Monroe. It's about 15 miles outside of Athens, Georgia which is the home of the UGA Bulldogs. To be honest, there is absolutely no motivation in Monroe for a young inspiring entrepreneur like myself, but I remember often going to downtown Atlanta. I admired the atmosphere. Seeing progressive mindset people starting businesses, living in luxury homes, and driving foreign cars always provoked me

HomeTown

2012 Olympic Champions

to stay focus and work hard for what I wanted. You have to find a place where you feel inspired as soon as you walk in the door and become energized. Areas like Downtown, Mid-town, and Buckhead help me to stay on track and work hard. Ironically, as I write this chapter, I am sitting in a Starbucks on PeachTree Street Midtown Atlanta. I don't know what it is, but being around people who look like they are doing something productive makes me more productive. I use to go to the library and buy poster boards and old magazines and make vision boards. A vision board is one big collage of pictures that reflects your desires in your future; this is an awesome form of motivation because it's a daily reminder of why you should keep pushing.

No matter what form of motivation works to get you going, just know that motivation births inspiration, inspiration sparks passion, and passion builds dreams. Recall, in chapter two, I said you have to be around the right people who believe in your dream in order to be motivated by them. Think about the relationships in your life, what motivates you about them? Do you motivate them?

Proverbs 27:17 says "As iron sharpens iron, so one person sharpens another." I absolutely love this bible verse because for one it's the only verse I can remember besides John 11:35 Jesus wept. and John 3:16. The proverb scripture is relevant to this chapter because it speaks volumes to the connection with relationships and motivation in your life. My cousin Troy quoted this verse after Usain Bolt, Warren Weir, and, Yohan Blake won first, second, and third place for Jamaica in the 2012 Olympics. This is a prime example of what working hard and pushing to boost each other will do, everyone will win!

So many people cheered for me at an early age. They guided me to pursue my dreams. Watching them perfect their craft also challenged me to try harder. You see, growing up, I use to be in a secret competition with my oldest sister Paula. Secret meaning, she never knew what was going on, but my jealously for her accomplishments excited me. My sister has always had this outstanding ability to connect with people and get what she wanted, whether it

Eldredge & Paula as kids   Eldredge & Paula as adults

was a job or promotion. Paula has a God- given gift of gab. She is a fashion guru and was voted most likely to succeed among all of my siblings. I hated that she was so good! All I wanted to do in life was beat her in everything! I remember when she got her license. Although, I was only twelve, I began to study for my learner's exam as if I had to take it the following day. When my parents bought her first car, I began to save money just so I could buy a better car one day. This happened all throughout our lives even now as adults. We still compete. Back in 2009, Paula and I both had a job at this small costume Jewelry store in Stonecrest Mall called Beautifi. Sales were kinda slow before we arrived, but when we started working, we competed with each other constantly. Not only did it make us driven, but store sales begin to increase. Competition has always been one of my main sources of motivation; I wanted to be the best or to be respected by the best.

In high school, two of my strongest relationships were with Dreco Bostic and Rashaud Tate. We all had athletic scholarships and played football for Athens Christian School. To be truthful with you, I don't know why they allowed me to play on the team. It was obvious why they picked Dreco and Rashaud. Dreco was the all American running back who ran as fast as lighting, hence me calling

him "Black Shadow." I called him "Mr. 339" too because
he ran for 339 yards in two quarters one game. Rashaud
was a defensive beast and probably the strongest athlete in
the school. He held multiple records in the schools' weight
room. He is known for squatting 550lbs, which is very
impressive. However, I was as much of a decorated athlete
as Michael Phelps. I was about 5'6 1/2, weighed 160lbs
soaking wet, and ran a five flat forty time (which isn't good).
But...I had heart and a great personality and obviously some
sort of leadership ability for them to keep me on the team. If
you ask me, they judged a book by the cover. But thank God
they did because attending that school helped me to build
some really strong relationships. My conclusion is I became
a better athlete because Dreco and Rashaud motivated me
to work diligently. Who pushes you to go further in life?
Who won't let you quit?

Becoming motivated is absolutely vital to become
M.A.D.E. Take a second and evaluate exactly where your
motivation levels are and then think about where you want
them to be. I am giving you this information because I know
it works. This is necessary, and I know you can do it. You
can change your family, your friends, your school, your
life or anything you put your mind to, when you become
motivated.

Steps to Become Motivated

Become established in your goals

Goals are guidelines that help you track your success.

Become surrounded by your motivation source

Discover what pushes you forward and keeps you going.

Become an apprentice

Find someone who has become successful in the field you desire go and make them your mentor.

Become attentive to your inner circles' motivation

See who motivates you in your circle and why? Or why not?

Become familiar with your incentives

Research the benefits of reaching your goals in life and use them as motivating incentives to keep going.

Please complete the following exercise. Please use pencil.

List 5 people who motivate you and why?

_____

_____

_____

_____

_____

_____

_____

_____

_____

_____

_____

_____

_____

_____

_____

_____

_____

_____

Create a vision board

Step 1

Buy materials such as post board, magazines (Library), and glue.

Step 2

Cut pictures out that reflect your desires for the future. (cars, houses, clothes, etc)

Step 3

Glue pictures on poster board until it has no more space available.

Step 4

Hang up on your wall or somewhere you will see it every day.

Step 5

Take a picture and email it to contact@becomemade.org we will put it on our website.

Chapter Four

Become An Adult

Before you read this chapter, I need to get something straight. I don't want anyone being cynical and taking the title of this chapter literal. Just because you are about to become M.A.D.E, doesn't mean you are grown now. What it does mean is that you are about to adopt the characteristics of an adult to your life. Meaning you are about to become more mature, make necessary sacrifices, and be respectful at all times. When attempting to build great relationships at a young age, there is a sense of maturity that must be developed. Becoming an adult will cause you to become more goal oriented, and you will begin to prioritize things better in life.

For example, I use to bump heads with my parents a lot because I wanted to do certain things and they wouldn't let me. If my mama said I couldn't go to a party, I would lie and say I'm going to a friend's house and then go to the party. As I got older, I started my journey of becoming M.A.D.E. I learned that in order to get the respect as a young adult from my parents I needed to respect myself. If I really felt like I was mature enough to go to the party, I would not be sneaking out of the house at night in order to go. Therefore, when I decided to become a young adult, I stopped lying. If my mama said "no, I couldn't go somewhere", I didn't talk back, nor smack my teeth, or even show a hint of an attitude. The only thing I did was say, "yes ma'am" and found something else to do at the house. Now, was this easy? No, not at all! I hated it actually! What happened over time was that my parents begin to see the growth in my maturity and they begin to allow me to do more. The first thing you have to learn about being an adult is you have to give respect to earn it. If the people around you really respected you, they would not allow you to disrespect yourself and others.

Secondly, an adult must have accountability. Accountability is the responsibility to someone or for some activity. Ok, the first part says responsibility to someone. Can you guess who that someone is? Yeah buddy, that's right, it's you! Regardless of what happens in life, you could become rich and famous or poor and homeless. The final outcome is completely up to you. It's easy to blame others for our mistakes in life, but it's a waste of time. Some of you might have some real stress on your shoulders. You're being raised in a single parent home, your family financial status may not be that good, or you may have been verbally or physically abused. I am not trying to minimize whatever your current situation is but I am telling you that the only thing that matters is the finish line. Go look at the vision board you just made (Please Do All Exercises). What is your ultimate goal? Everything that does not line up with that goal is considered to be sideline drama. The only way you are going to be successful is if you learn to focus on what matters. If you have affluent relationships in your life, they will not allow you to feel sorry for yourself or misuse time. Their overall goal is to see you succeed. Real friends will hold you accountable for your actions. It may get on your last nerve, but you will thank them in the end.

The second part of the word accountability means to be responsible for some activity. It's important that you learn this now because these are principles that will assist you throughout your adult life. For example: "I am failing my math class because my teacher doesn't know how to teach" or "my boss is tripping and getting on me for no reason and I didn't do anything," These are excuses so you won't be held accountable. The truth of the matter is the root of everything you experience can be pointed back to you. When you learn to do this, you will not squander your life trying to find out who to blame. Rather, you will instantly learn to look for the solution to the problem and that my friend is showing signs of you becoming an adult. What else does becoming an adult mean? It means that everything might not go the way you think it should, but you have to learn to comply with every situation and move forward. I learned this by watching my two phenomenal little sisters, Winnie and Victoria. For the most part, my parents were always around and available for me. I was home-schooled for most of my life and even when I went to regular school, my parents were still accessible. I can't say the same for my little sisters. In 2009, my dad decided to take his company in a different direction. The good news is he was successful and it took him to a wealthy place, but the bad news was it required both parents to move away from Georgia. At that time, Winnie was in her junior year and Victoria was still in eighth grade. To make sure that their grades weren't affected; my parents decided that my sisters should stay in Georgia with me. This caused a major adjustment in all our lives, but mainly for them because my parents would not be so readily on hand in a very critical

Eldredge & The Girls   The Girls

time of their lives. At first, it was a full-time headache for me because at the age of twenty, I was expected to be the legal guardian of two teenage girls. In my head, I was their new daddy and in their head, I was the over protective big brother who kept getting on their nerves. Most people would have taken this opportunity to make excuses, and probably even act out of character. However, they did just the opposite. My little sisters worked hard and stayed focus on their grades. Was it easy for them? Of course not! It was constant confrontation, but always climaxed down to peace. We made it through and survived every situation.

My sisters are successful in everything they do because they choose to apply the concept of M.A.D.E in their personal lives. Winnie now attends Lincoln University in Pennsylvania. She understands the theory of building prominent relationships. Winnie has succeeded in gaining a powerful influence with her student body and with the President now she is the SGA President of her school. Best of all, she is also very active mentor of M.A.D.E and serves as a mentor to middle and high school students all over the world. Victoria moved to Oklahoma City with our parents her sophomore year. When she first got there, she did not know anyone. But she quickly made a great name for herself by getting involved in the community. I was very proud of her progress because Victoria has always been shy around new people; however, being in a new state away from her older siblings, pushed her to build new relations. Victoria's new found confidence enabled her to become the first place recipient of the Oklahoma ArtScience Award. Oklahoma was selected as the second US site for the ArtScience Prize, an international creativity project for young people developed by a Harvard professor. This inspired her to establish her own organization "Measureless Hope" which she plans on bringing radical change to her community in Oklahoma City. As you can see, I am very pleased with my sisters, they applied the M.A.D.E principles of becoming an adult. Now, it's your turn.

Winnie Washington

Victoria Washington

Steps to Become an Adult

Become disciplined

Decide that you are going to stay focused on your goal.

Become willing to make sacrifices

Choose the people and/or habits you have to sacrifice in order to get you closer to your goal.

Become like your mentor

Analyze your mentor's success patterns then begin to adapt them to your personal life.

Become receptive to an image adjustment

Make any necessary changes to your image that will help you progress.

Become more developed in your dialogue

Begin to speak in a more mature way which will help build your communication skills.

Please complete the following exercise. Please use pencil.

Do you feel you take responsibility for your action?
Why or why not?

_____

_____

_____

_____

_____

_____

_____

_____

_____

Name one mentor you feel you should mimic. Explain.

_____

_____

_____

_____

_____

_____

_____

_____

_____

3 areas in your life you feel you should add maturity?

_____

_____

_____

_____

_____

_____

_____

_____

_____

_____

_____

_____

_____

_____

_____

_____

_____

_____

_____

_____

_____

_____

_____

_____

_____

Chapter
Five
Become Developed

Ghandi once said, "Be the change you wish to see in the world." This quote is very profound and it can also be applied to our lives. Everything you have read in this book sounds good, but it means absolutely nothing if you do not begin to practice these concepts daily. When you grabbed this book, you may have had some thoughts to make a change in your life. Now it's time to follow through. Have you been true to yourself? Do you think you are motivated? Do you feel you are being a mature young adult? Hopefully, you answered yes to these questions, but if not, now is the time to begin preparing yourself. When you become M.A.D.E, you and the people around you will begin to see the transition. To become developed means to become the change you wish to see. You must start to make your mentality your reality. The way you think must become the way you act. If you desire to be a professional football player, you must begin working out, eating, and developing yourself like a professional football player now. You must form habits and establish an inner circle that will compliment and support your dreams. In order to become developed, it will take much endurance, work, and discipline.

When it comes to making decisions and becoming developed, my older brother Nick wins the gold. The crazy thing about Nick is we look exactly alike and have a lot of the similar features; however, Nick was adopted when I was twelve- years- old. Nick did not come from the best background. Most people would say that he had a very rough childhood, but he did not allow his upbringing to hold him back. The first time I met Nick was at Milledgeville Youth Detention Center. At the center, the church youth group held outreach sermons and basketball competitions. We lost every game we played. Despite of our constant defeat, we started building strong relationships and that's how I met Nick. When he came home from Milledgeville, he was determined to bring a positive change to his life. Church In The Now had a program (Now House) that provided work and shelter for young boys who were recently released from jail.

My entire family built a true bond with Nick because he was with us all the time. This was heaven for me because I finally had the brother I always wanted. We were inseparable, where he went, I went, what he wore, I wore. The only reason why I talk to older women now is because I was forced to talk to friends of Nick's girlfriend I was twelve and he was sixteen at the time. The thing I admire most about Nick is that I never heard him give excuses for his life. Nick never gave up. He graduated high school when he was sixteen and enrolled into college immediately at seventeen. I do not know anyone who has as much discipline as my brother. My sisters and I all sang background for my mom, but unfortunately Nick didn't have the natural gift. So, while attending school at Gordon College, Nick self- taught himself how to play the guitar by watching youtube videos. Today, Nick is a talented musician and a phenomenal lyricist. He taught me how to rap. Nick made a decision to change and he began to develop everything in his life to fit that change. You have to do the same thing. Everything around you must point in the direction you are headed. The choice is in your hands. In life, there are two types of people. The ones who talk about it and the ones who make it happen. You may feel like you're overwhelmed with everything that is going on in your life, but what other

Don Nick Luciano

Nick teaching students music

choice do you have. Are you going to give up? Seriously? No! You have to get up and get focused on to the finish line. If the people around you are not pushing you, it means two things: either they are not motivated or they don't care. I cannot stress this point enough. Your circle of influence will impact you to do good or bad. My challenge to you is to stop making excuses for yourself, stop being lazy, stop being scared, stop doubting yourself, stop holding yourself back and get out of your own way! You were built for this and you will be able to undergo whatever obstacle that comes in your way. I believe in you! It's now time that you believe in yourself and become developed into the astronomical person you were born to be.

Steps to Become Developed

Become a product of your mentality

Think like you have already reached your goals.

Become the manifestation of your good habits

Change your bad habits and develop good ones.

Become focused on your Plan

Create a road map so you can clearly see where you're going.

Become a positive person

Developed a positive attitude and don't feel sorry for yourself. Always think positive.

Become disciplined

You have to become patient and focus on your goals.

Please complete the following exercise. Please use a pencil.

List 3 bad habits you wish to change in order to reach you goal?

_____

_____

_____

_____

_____

_____

_____

_____

_____

List skills you must learn in order to advance your goals?

_____

_____

_____

_____

_____

_____

_____

Develop a plan to help you accomplish the two tasks above.

_____

_____

_____

_____

_____

_____

_____

_____

_____

_____

_____

_____

_____

_____

_____

_____

_____

_____

_____

_____

_____

_____

Chapter
Six
Become Excellence

This chapter is for the winners! To become M.A.D.E. means to become excellent in every part of your life. "If better is an option, then good is not enough." This is a quote from Ida Mae Howard. Amusingly, this is my grandmother's maiden name, but unfortunately I can't give her the credit for this quote. I want you to take a second and think to yourself, can I do better? The truth is we all can do better. Your goal should be to strive for excellence in everything you do. The people in your life right now can either allow you to be content and accept mediocrity or they will push you to excel. I have experienced both types of people. There is no greater feeling than having someone in your corner that is going to push you towards success.

James Flanagan was my first boss. He gave me a job at the age of fourteen with his bus company, Boswell Motor Coach. I learned so much while working with Mr. James. He taught me to be excellent at my job. My duty was to wash the buses and he didn't cut me any slack. I had to check under every seat, look in every compartment, and scrub the bathrooms until the bus looked brand new. I was able to travel everywhere with the bus and meet many people. I remember telling Mr. James, I wanted to get my CDL and drive buses like he did. Yet, he told me no. I was shocked at his response, so I quickly asked him why? He told me that

47

I had a gift and that I was talented enough to do whatever I wanted in life. Driving buses would be fun, but it would not have done my potential any justice. That stuck with me over the years. I still go to Mr. James for advice on everything; he has become like family to me.

Another person who pushed me to do more in life was Mr. Doug Hauptman. I was seventeen years old when I met him. He often volunteered at my church youth service. I had just made a decision to dress differently. I gave away all of my jeans, shorts, sneakers, pretty much everything causal and I wore nothing but slacks with a shirt and tie every day. Again, I am not implying that you have to be as extreme as I was to adjust your image. It worked for me, I'm just saying. Imagine this good looking young kid running around in the youth service (back then it was called Teen Planet) playing basketball in his Sunday's best, getting sweaty and looking a hot mess. I am pretty sure it was easy for me to stand out in the crowd. What I didn't know was Mr. Doug was quietly watching me every week. One Wednesday night, he pulled me to the side and asked me, "Why you always dressed up?" I smiled and simply responded, "Because it makes me look and feel good." Doug laughed while he pulled his card out of his pocket and said, "Do you have a job?" I was surprised because I knew that dressing like this made me stand out, but I didn't think it would get me a job too. Doug told me to meet him at his office next week to discuss more details of the opening position. I reported to his office; bright and early. I was so excited because I was about to get a new job. I didn't know what to expect. I recalled going into the interview and Doug immediately asked me, "What do you have to offer and why do you want this job?"

Looking confused, I thought to myself, why is he asking me these questions. He asked me to come here not the other way around. I was nervous and timid trying to give off the perception of a mature young adult. He didn't seem convinced, but he still hired me. The first thing I noticed about this job was that it is a completely different world than working with Mr. James. Doug was the owner of Office Pavillion Suites. He hired me to be a sales rep. My duties as a sales rep was to get business owners to either rent an office from us or purchase any of our services such as websites, business cards, graphic design and more. Man, I loved that job! I had to dress up every day, had my own office, and a company laptop. I was the youngest working person in the building. Both Mr. James and Doug's teaching methods were different. Mr. James was very caring and took his time to walk me through each step. On the other hand, Doug threw me in the water and said "swim." I literally sat in my office for the first two days on Facebook and played solitaire because I didn't know what to do. Doug didn't go easy based of my age. He wanted results and pushed me to be the best. He also showed me that being excellent does not have an age limit, but is measured by your work ethic. It built my confidence so much that I quit and decided to start my own business with my cousin Troy. Unfortunately, the business didn't take off like I needed; therefore, I had to go get a job at McDonald's to make ends meet. My point is that Doug did not allow me to be an average seventeen year old. He recognized the excellence in me. When you surround yourself with great relationships, there is no way to stay normal because everyone around you will be progressing and they will not leave you behind.

There are so many people that I can name who have entered into my life and pushed me to be who I am today. Rick Johnson, friend and mentor, stands above all the rest. His tremendous guidance has made lasting impacts on my life. I was working at Stonecrest Mall moving from store to store because I was always looking for better opportunities. At the time, I was working at Sunglass Hut and Rick was the manager of Littman Jewelers next door. I have always been a loquacious person full of zeal; I use to talk to everyone who worked in the mall because I considered myself to be the mayor. I had no intent of trying to work at Littman Jewelers, thus you can imagine my surprise when Rick offered me a job. While working with Rick, he inspired me to become excellent in my customer service, product knowledge, and professionalism. Littman Jewelers was the last job I held before deciding to be a full time entrepreneur and focus on M.A.D.E. Rick knew my passion was not in jewelry, but he believed in me and allowed my work schedule to be flexible. I left several times thinking I was ready to be on my own, but when I realized I was mistaken, he still accepted me back without chastising me for my ignorance. Rick was by far the coolest manager I have ever had to work for. That's the reason why I stayed at Littman Jewelers for so long. Before working with Rick, I averaged a solid 2 - 4 months on every job. I worked at Littman

Eldredge & Mr. Rick Johnson

Eldredge & Mr. James

Jewelers for 2 years.

My older sister Shardia showed me the concept of becoming excellent in life through the peer perspective. Since Shardia was a young girl, she always wanted to dance and be a cheerleader. I watched her work hard to develop her God- given gift and how she advanced herself. She has performed on multiple platforms including recreational, middle and high school, college (FAMU University), and hereafter on a professional level. She is now a member of the Charlotte Hornets dance team because she stayed true and focused on her passion. Shardia showed me that practice does make perfect and hard work will pay off in the end. She has been a great example to me. Like all of my siblings, I am grateful they are part of my life.

These are a few examples of people who caused me to be superlative. To become excellent, you have to perform above the average Joe. You cannot settle for less in life. Don't become an athlete, become an excellent athlete. Don't become an average student, become an excellent student. In order to become excellent, you have to take pride in everything you do. Your name is the only thing you will have when it's all said and done, so make it stand for something when people mention you.

When I was thinking of the acronym for M.A.D.E, I could

have made the E stand for anything. I chose excellence because I wanted to set the standard for the people I allowed in my life. I realized that the relationships I held played a major role in the outcome of my success story. Once you begin to challenge yourself to apply excellence in every part of your life, you will begin to see a tremendous difference. When it comes to negative relationships, they will not stay around long because misery loves company. When you begin to elevate yourself, they will not rise up with you unless they too are ready to become M.A.D.E.

Eldredge & Shardia

Shardia as a Lady Cat

Steps to Become Excellence

Become a student 24/7

Listen to your parents, teachers, and mentors and gain the wisdom they have to offer.

Become receptive to constructive criticism

Do not be offended when someone corrects you or give you an alternative suggestion.

Become distinguished

Stand out in a positive way. Build your brand by always being different from the crowd.

Become proud

Take pride in absolutely everything that you do.

Become the standard

Raise the bar and become the standard that students want to live up to.

Please complete the following exercise. Please use a pencil.

Where in your life do you feel you can improve and do better?

_____

_____

_____

_____

_____

_____

_____

_____

List one person in your life who has pushed you to do better and how?

_____

_____

_____

_____

_____

_____

_____

Do you feel you stand out from the crowd? If so, why? If not, why not?

_____

_____

_____

_____

_____

_____

_____

_____

_____

_____

_____

_____

_____

_____

_____

_____

_____

_____

_____

Chapter
Seven

Become the M.A.D.E. Generation

The M.A.D.E lifestyle is a higher living through building prosperous relationships that will successfully help you reach your goals. Although the concept of becoming M.A.D.E may be new to you right now, you have heard of the M.A.D.E Generations throughout history. A generation that gains a forward mindset and they discover their purpose as a whole is considered to be the M.A.D.E Generation. Whenever a group of motivated young adults come together to develop excellence, they always make history. In order to become the M.A.D.E Generation, you have to focus on yourself as an individual. Then start to tune-in on your peers as a whole. Once you identify your piece, you can then discover where you belong in the puzzle.

Dr. Martin Luther King Jr. may be the best example I can think of when it comes to starting a M.A.D.E Generation. He discovered his purpose in life and he realized where he could help his generation. The results of the Civil Rights movement made a major impact in their lifetime and we are still reaping the benefits of their hard work. The fascinating thing about the Civil Rights movement was how young the people were. Dr. Martin Luther King Jr was very motivated at a young age and always strived for excellence. His hard work and determination was clearly seen. He graduated from high school at 15 and became the youngest man to ever receive the Nobel Peace Prize at 35. That's only two of the many incredible accomplishments of Dr. King. He gained many followers because he led by example. He knew what he believed and stayed true to himself.

Bottom line, the MLK generation became M.A.D.E and they changed the world. I believe that our generation now has been called to do something great, but unfortunately we do not know our purpose. See, we have a lot of great achievements that other generations attempted, but were not successful. The technology industry has reached pinnacle heights. For example, the cell phone can now do more than a computer could do ten years ago. Our imagination and creativity has removed the limits and developed resources that have altered mankind. One of my favorite accomplishments of our generation is that we elected the first black President. Whether you agree with his tactics or not is irrelevant. President Barack Obama represents progression. So many people laid down their lives, so he could have this opportunity. Our generation has managed to do all of this and we are completely unorganized. Imagine if we could get it together people? Think for a moment, if everyone focused on their individual purpose we will discover our purpose as a whole. I believe once we stop being idle and do what's important, we will be able to become a M.A.D.E. Generation and we will go down in history.

Our generation is currently focused on nothing but trends. I personally blame the media, but I would need another book to explain my opinion on that. Can you call to mind when we use to wear our clothes three sizes to big? Suddenly, after the futuristic trend, everyone was rushing to American Eagle and Abercrombie to buy small shirts and skinny jeans. There is a saying that says, "If you stand for nothing you will fall for anything." What are we standing for? What are we trying to do? What is our purpose? You cannot answer these questions for your generation until you can answer these questions for yourself first. It takes unity to find purpose and goals to reach dreams. In order

Eldredge coaching during mentor sessions

to reach the next level we all want to see, we have to begin to take accountability for each other. This is why I founded M.A.D.E. I wanted to create an atmosphere that made it easy to connect with people who wanted to bring change in the world. M.A.D.E is geared toward middle and high school students because I feel like these are the two most crucial stages of a young person's life. In middle school, I began to feel like I had an idea of who I was and in high school, I began to completely develop into that person. The more knowledge, insight, and wisdom you receive in these two stages of your life, the better you will be when you move on to the next stage. I chose to use college students and young professionals for my mentors because I know that they have something to offer that no one else can. College students and young professionals (early twenties to early thirty's) are young enough to stay connected, but old enough to be respected.

I knew that M.A.D.E was an idea that I wanted to share with the world, so I created a plan that could be simply and easily duplicated. Soon M.A.D.E will be launching chapters on colleges and universities across the nation. The goal of every M.A.D.E chapter is to build more community involvement while helping students discover their purpose through rich relationships. M.A.D.E will strive to provide positive entertainment, education, and mentoring for the surrounding middle and high school students. The desired outcome of every M.A.D.E. chapter is to restore the family structure in the community. I believe that the traditional family image has been altered; therefore, my goal is to show our community a new successful model. I hope to one day offer every individual who joins M.A.D.E. a group of people they can call family. The intent of M.A.D.E is not to bring together a targeted group based on age, gender, race, religion, or background, but to bring unity by breaking down all social barriers in our community. My ultimate goal for establishing M.A.D.E in various parts of the world is to raise up a generation of true leaders who have strong character, innovative minds, and moral standards.

When I became M.A.D.E, I decided to surround myself with people who I saw striving for success and who I knew would hold me liable for my actions. The only way we are going to be champions are if we begin to work together and push each other forward. The time is now for us to rise up against the statistics of being a lost generation. You can start now by getting your friends, cousins, classmates, teammates, absolutely everyone you know to become M.A.D.E and start exercising these principles to your lifestyle. This will not be an easy task, but it's compelled to work. As I stated in the beginning, I wrote this book as a road map to help you navigate your way through each relationships you encounter. Take these steps seriously, apply them and I guarantee you will see a positive change in yourself. So, I challenge you this day to become M.A.D.E because it's a lifestyle worth living.

Eldredge & Beau
aka Lil Ice Cream Dude

Eldredge at Dream Keepers MLK
Center Camping Trip

Steps to Become the M.A.D.E Generation

Become accountable for your relationships

Become accountable to the people in your life and help them stay focused.

Become united by your purpose

Identify like-minded people who believe in your mission and become united by your purpose.

Become supporter of leaders

Support individuals in your generation who have decided to focus on bringing change. You never know they may be the next great leader.

Become trendsetters

In the words of my good friend Kenshu Aoki President of GPYC – USA "Break the trend and build the future."

Become a part of the M.A.D.E Movement

Join the M.A.D.E movement by visiting www.becomemade.org.

Please complete the following exercise. Please use a pencil.

What do you think our generation purpose is?

_____

_____

_____

_____

_____

_____

_____

Who do you feel are the young leaders of our generation?

_____

_____

_____

_____

_____

_____

_____

_____

_____

_____

_____

_____

_____

What do you feel you have to offer to our generation's purpose?

_____

_____

_____

_____

_____

_____

_____

_____

_____

_____

_____

_____

_____

_____

List 3 people you feel you should buy a copy of this book?

_____

_____

_____

_____

_____

About The Author

Eldredge E. Washington also known as Made Mann believes in three things: God, family, and community. At the age of 18 he decided to dedicate his life to rebuilding and installing back the pride into our communities. He relentlessly invested all of his time, energy, and resources into founding M.A.D.E (Motivated Adults Developing Excellence); which is one of the most innovative and supportive group mentoring non-profit organizations in Atlanta, GA. Eldredge's secret to the success of his organization is building strong relationships. The electrifying love that Eldredge leaves in the hearts of those he encounters is undeniable. With his affectionate spirit he uplifts everyone who crosses his path. Eldredge is on a mission to help his generation progress by coaching them on how to live the M.A.D.E lifestyle. Eldredge has traveled domestically and internationally spreading the message of "Become M.A.D.E." He believes if you see more and want more, you will eventually do more with the support from the people in your life. Ultimately, Eldredge desires to coach people on healthy relationships building which will help them discover purpose and accomplish goals in their life. When asked about the uncannily behavior of his generation, Eldredge stated a quote from author Stephen Covey, "If you want to change someone's behavior, you change their title." Instead of complaining about the high school drop outs, teen mothers, gang members and drug dealers, Eldredge has decided to change their title to the leaders of tomorrow. Eldredge encourages everyone to Become M.A.D.E. because it's a lifestyle worth living.

Book Acknowledgements

I can honestly say that writing this book was a lot easier than I thought it would be. Once I began to write the words literally flowed effortlessly from my thoughts onto the paper. The only time I faced a challenge throughout this entire process was writing this acknowledgement. This was an issue because I have so many people that I want to thank for helping me to get focused and become M.A.D.E. I would need an entire book to name everyone who has contributed to my success story. I would like to apologize in advance to anyone who may be left out, your support is very valued and I am forever thankful.

First, I would like to acknowledge my parents Eldredge and Paulette Washington. I know I dedicated the book to you both, but I cannot express how grateful I am for all that you do for me. You two are simply perfect and I could not ask for better parents.

Secondly, I would like to acknowledge my siblings Paula, Shardia, Nick, Winnie, and Victoria. I really don't think I have ever expressed how much you guys motivate me to keep going. I am so proud of all of you because I see the way you pursue your passion in life and that is truly inspiring. I attempted to acknowledge you all in the book but that does our relationship and your value in my life no justice. You all are absolutely phenomenal and I thank you for all of your continued support. I promise you that this is only the beginning and you will soon reap the benefits because I am doing this for us!

I would like to thank Isaiah Galloway for being the most amazing nephew that an uncle could have. You are a very smart kid and I am excited to see how great you will become. Thank you for believing in me and always making me feel like your hero.

To my grandparents Albert Floyd, Winnie Floyd (RIP), Evelyn Floyd, Pop and Ida Washington thank you for everything you have done for me. I love you all and I am working very hard to make you all proud.

I want to thank all of my aunts and uncles for all of the life lessons that you all have taught me through lectures, personal examples, and hands on experiences. You all have played a major role in my life and I thank you for believing in your FAVORITE nephew. Unfortunately, I have completely too many cousins to name in this acknowledgement, but I want to specifically highlight a few who have really inspired me either by encouragement or just example. First I want to acknowledge hands down my favorite cousin on both sides Troy J. Wilson II! Many people do not know this but my cousin Troy is the mastermind behind my entire empire. He has supported me since day one with insight, ideas, and his much needed skill set. I just want to thank you for always being there when I need you to be there. Also, I want to thank Chantell (his wife) for allowing him to stay up late designing different projects that I needed done. I love you and your family more than you will ever know. Next I have to give a shout out to Tiffany aka Titty-Face, Victoria and Lil' Morris, Harrison aka Chucky, Crystal and Jarrad Blade, Marquis, Marcus, and Andria Floyd.

I would like to thank all of my mentors who have and continue to sow into my life selflessly. Rick Johnson, James Flanagan, Gerald Alphin, Dr. Paul Murray, Al Addae,

Derrick Bozeman, Mawuli Davis, Ron Love, and last but not least Marcus Larry Griffin.

To the amazing board of directors of the M.A.D.E organization; Morgan Bryant, Bridgette Mitchell, Marsha Shackelford, Minh Van, Mike Ryan, AJ Vassar and Febra Clark. The world is not ready for the work we are about to do with M.A.D.E. Together I know we will be a spark that will start a wild fire of change in our community. Thank you for believing in me and thank you for never giving up on our mission.

The following list contains names of friends who have courageously stood by me as I fault the good fight in the trenches of our community. There are many people who I have built relationships with during the journey of starting the M.A.D.E organization, but these are the ones who have supported me way more than a friend could ever ask for. Dawn Griffin (your support is the fuel that keeps me going), Collin Nunez (my oldest friend, thank you for your genuine friendship), Levi Dickerson, Jahan Vahid, David Tooms, Alvin Jenekins aka AJP, Janell Braxton aka Dr.

Braxton, Noelle Singleton, Rashedia Neal, Kendon Kelley, Angelo Lopera, Travis Stegall (Thank you for exposing the dolphin), Chris Freeman, Ray aka Phame, Marlon Williams, Shaun Mathis, Tarnisha Thomas, Minister Tanisha Moore, John and Terrie Elmore, Lloyd W. Sutton (Thank you for teaching me how to Run With It), Tiffany Wills (you are so amazing thank you for feeding my mind and body), Anana Parris (Thank you for teaching me the importance of Self Care), Judah Swilley (this is the year we win the Super Bowl), Jonah Swilley (Thank you for always being willing to help me succeed bro, I can't wait to see you make it) Sam Collier (don't stop WINNING bro), Josh Mosley (thank you for being a brother and making sure I graduated high school), Rodney Price (you're the man and you always will be), Bridgette Zulu (you are growing into an amazing young leader), Lamontrey Allen aka Iman (you are one of the most intelligent students I have ever encountered. Thank you for allowing me to help you on your journey of success.), Tavaughn Wynche aka Sway (you were born to lead and succeed in every area of your life. Never stop being

M.A.D.E), Eunique Swain (I have watched you climb this mountain of life and I intend on watching you reach the top, so let's do it together). DJ Vitamo, Alma G. Davis (the only reason I used that name is because you are the original Diva), DJ E Double U, Tia O'Connor, Erica Thomas (you always have my vote), Candice McKinley, Jean Hudley, Candace Reece, Tereance Puryear, DJ MVP, Stephen Churn, Jasper Boykin Jr. aka G, Stevie Baggs, Ms. Jewel (my second mama), Brian, Terrilyn, Ms. Crystal Flanagan, Rita and Trina Striker, Desha Elliott, Iesha Akyempong, Fly Musiq, Jewel Alexander, Kenshu Aoki, Kimi, Nathan, and the whole GPF Family, Stevie Baggs (thank you for teaching me how to be greater than the game), Karega Bailey (you are the key to the music revolution continue to give life through lyrics), Ink and Joe aka Vintage Nation, Kristina Wynn, Martin Banks, Ben Grey, Kimberly Banks, Antwon Davis, Big Country the owner of Bigg Country BBQ, Dreco Bostic, Alex Brown aka Trell, JC Culbreath, Xavier Gordon, Lauren and Shaina Johnson, Alexander Griffin, Jonathan Kennebrew, Jay Bailey, Blair and Michele Caplinger, Mary

Render (this book would not be here if it was not for you! Thank you for all the long night reading and editing each chapter with me. You are truly God's sent Angel), Mesheka Carson aka Lady Ice, Martin Kumi (we about to really change the world with shoes now), Louis and Caleb Deas, and Frank Battle (words cannot express how much your support has made this possible. Thank you for being my brother and thank you for teaching me how to be a king).

Lastly, I would like to thank Howard Clay for being a true brother, friend, and supporter. You have truly given me the best gift that anyone could ever give me and that is the gift of opportunity. Thank you for taking a big risk and making a huge investment by publishing my first book. I promise you that we will make an impact like no other with this project. Continue to teach the world how to be a B.O.S.S.!

CPSIA information can be obtained at www.ICGtesting.com
Printed in the USA
LVOW05s0535191214

419566LV00006B/9/P